The *Zen* of Programming

edited and translated by

Geoffrey James

with an Introduction by
Charlie Babbage

and a Foreword by
Doctor C. P. Yu

INFO
BOOKS

The Zen of Programming

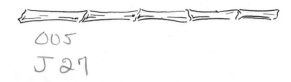

OUS
J 27

© 1988 by Geoffrey James
Published by InfoBooks
P. O. Box 1018, Santa Monica, CA 90406

Cover design and illustration: Gloria Garland
Text design and illustrations: Gloria Garland
Japanese calligraphy: Teri Fujikawa

Printed in the United States of America

10 9 8 7 6 5 4 3 2 1

ISBN 0-931137-09-8

INFO

BOOKS

P.O. Box 1018
Santa Monica
California 90406
213-470-6786

Dedication

For my Mother

The Zen of Programming

Preface

The publication of *The Tao of Programming* (InfoBooks, 1987) was so well received by the programming public that I was asked by InfoBooks to present a translation of the peripheral and related texts that serve to complement the famous classic. Although I protested that my abilities were inadequate to the task, I was at length persuaded to attempt it.

The present volume is the result of many months of study and translation. It attempts to encapsulate a complex subject through the presentation of exerpts from the traditional source works. I have

little doubt that many compuar-
cheologists will question my selections. "Why did he not include
the parable of The Unix* Programm-
mer, the Elephant, and the Prosti-
tute," they will ask, or "How dare
he neglect the time-honored tale
of Turing's Adventures in Mar-
ketingland!" To these critics I can
only say that I have done my best
to make a representative selection.

To date the various passages in the
text, I have utilized the dynasty
system. For those not familiar
with this method of dating, there
have been been four dynasties or
"generations."

---

*Unix is a trademark of Bell Labs.

The first dynasty, the so-called "golden age," harkens back to the days when computers were constructed of glass tubes; most modern scholars have concluded that this era is mythical. The second dynasty begins with the invention of the transistor and ends with the invention of the printed circuit.

Modern computer history begins with the third dynasty, which was dominated by mainframes and the warlords who controlled them. The fourth generation begins with the supression of the "Integration Sect," whose rebellion against the established order was brutally crushed by the fanatical "blue legion." Ironically, it was this sup-

pression that led to the spread of Zen programming into the outside world.

In addition to the traditional material that makes up the body of the present volume, I have been fortunate enough to secure the assistance of Drs. Babbage and Yu, who were kind enough to provide an Introduction and Foreword respectively. It is my hope that their contributions to this work will in some small way serve to overcome my inadequacies as the editor.

Geoffrey James
Los Angeles
January, 1988

Contents

This volume is organized into five books, following the ancient principle that divides the world into the five elements:

	Wood	Fire	Earth	Metal	Water
Master:	Ninjei	Noa-Op	Rinzai	Lan-Hsi	Yoshiko
Medium:	Chronicle 歷史	Folktale 昔話	Analect 俳句	Koan 講話	Haiku 說教
Hardware:	Keyboard	Monitor	CPU	Printer	Disk
Direction:	East	South	Center	West	North
Software:	Editor	Formatter	Debugger	Interpreter	Compiler
Sense:	Touch	Sight	Smell	Hearing	Taste
Phase:	Interface	Design	Coding	Debugging	Testing
Beast:	Dragon	Phoenix	Ox	Rabbit	Snake
System:	VMS	CP-6	OS/VS	MS-DOS	Unix

This system of classification is far too involved to be explained in a volume of this size. Meditation on the various correspondences sometimes reveals surprising insights.

Foreword

There is little doubt that the ancient art of programming is generally misunderstood by the Western mind. Popular opinion considers it a type of engineering, mechanistic and materialistic.

Many people believe that programming is merely a means to an end and that a program (and a programmer) can only be judged by the ability to make money.

These primitive misconceptions come from a profound misunder-

standing of the true purpose of programming.

The superior programmer does not strive for surface accomplishments but seeks a mystical identification between human and machine.

In the light of Zen, there is no separation between hardware, firmware, software, interface, and comprehension — rather all these are combined into an harmonious whole.

Attaining this state is only possible when the programmer has finally learned to set aside the false sense of ego with which most of us live our lives.

Foreword

This is *Computer-Dö* — the way of the Zen programmer.

It is sometimes said that a programmer who has mastered Zen has mastered life. Such a programmer views the world with an inexhaustible, childlike joy.

Walking down the street the enlightened programmer can sense the computers in the houses and buildings on either side.

The enlightened programmer can feel and hear the steady hum of the electrical pulses of modulated data transmission flowing through the telephone wires.

The enlightened programmer has become one with the universe.

As a teacher I am naturally gratified that my former pupil Geoffrey has been able to perform so great a service as to bring the lost classics of Zen programming to light.

It is to be hoped that this volume will reestablish Zen as an essential part of the well-rounded programmer's education.

Dr. C.P. Yu
College of Machine Transcendence,
Lotus University,
Llassa, Tibet

Introduction

When Mr. James asked me to provide an introduction to his next book, I could think of no better way to accomplish this than to relate my own personal experiences in the arcane realm of program maintenance, one of the least understood of the deadly arts of programming.

I do not doubt that some readers will maintain there there is little in common between the profound teachings of Zen and the humble art of program maintenance. But as the master said, "The way or path (Tao) is in all programs, even

in a video game." Therefore, it must also be true that the long-neglected art of program maintenance must have its Zen aspects, though they might not be immediately apparent to the untrained mind.

My story begins a few weeks after I had graduated from college with a bachelor's degree in computer science. My goal upon graduating was to work for a research and development organization, preferably in compiler or operating system design. I finally found an organization that was willing to hire me, but only on the condition that I "learn the system" by performing

program maintenance for an un-
specified period of time.

Naturally, I was somewhat offend-
ed at this suggestion. I had not
gone through five years of college
just to waste my time fixing some
other programmer's mistakes!
However, there was the promise
of interesting work in the future,
so I accepted, making a mental
note that I could always find another job if this one did not work
out.

When I reported to work the next
week, I was taken to meet the master of the maintenance group. The
personnel manager led me, quick
step, through the darkened corridors of the development center,

finally pointing out a door at the end of a long hallway. "He's in there," she said and then scurried away as if ill-at-ease.

I walked to the doorway and peered inside. I saw a man working at a terminal, but his back was towards me, so I had no idea of his age or appearance. I was just about make my presence known by coughing, when without as much as a single backward glance, the master said, "Please be seated."

I peered over his shoulder at the incomprehensible displays that flashed upon his terminal as his slender fingers danced across the keyboard. Finally, he gave a little

grunt of satisfaction, logged off, and then turned to face me.

What I saw surprised me, for he did not seem to be the type of man who would be a Zen master. His face was bland, almost ugly, and his hair formed a confused nimbus about his head. But what one noticed first were his eyes, which showed pale blue even through his thick spectacles.

He inspected me from head to foot and nodded, as if confirming a private opinion. "So you are the new-hire?" he asked sourly.

"Yes," I replied and, simulating an enthusiasm I did not feel, I gave

him a quick rundown of my experiences and grades in college.

The master listened politely and
then said, "That is all well and
good, but have you ever done program maintenance?"

I confessed that I had not.

The master heaved a great sigh.
"Well, we shall do what we can,"
he said. Then he took an enor-
mous program listing from a
shelf. Opening it at random, he
handed it to me and asked, "What
do you make of this?"

I stared at the listing. It was assem-
bly code intermingled with some

strange macro language. Every tenth line transferred control to some cryptic subroutine and if there was any structure to the program, it was incomprehensible to me. "What is this program?" I asked.

The master took the listing from my lap. "It is The Code of the Ancient Masters," he said, "And when you have learned to snatch the error code from the trap frame, it will be time for you to leave." Then he closed the listing and returned it to the shelf.

I soon learned that program maintenance was more difficult than I had assumed. I first attempted to

learn the assembler in which the Code had been written, but much to my annoyance, I discovered that the assembler had never been properly documented. All that existed was a set of notes from the hardware developers, who had died or left the company many years before.

The Code was of little help. It is true that there were occasional comments, but these were as opaque as the assembler, containing nothing but tantalizing references to primeval hardware architecture.

When I complained to the master, he listened politely, created a long

moment of silence between us and then answered me.

"You are seeking to understand something that cannot be understood by your rational mind," he said, "All that results is frustration. You must empty your mind. Only then will you come to understand The Code."

And the master began, slowly at first, to explain the convoluted logic of the The Code of the Ancient Masters. And as I listened to his calm and passive voice, I finally began to perceive a glimmer of the vast and eternal light that was hidden inside the Code. "The ancients knew nothing about 'good

programming practice'," the master said, "They sought to understand the inner workings of the universal 'computer-mind'. What need did they have for proper documentation? The programs were expressions of the ultimate."

But though I was slowly coming to understand, I felt as if I were a fly struggling in amber. So much of what the master said went against what I had learned, so little of it made sense to my rational mind. But the master was always patient with me, explaining again and again that I must stop trying to think with my rational mind, but rather to apprehend the meaning of the Code subconsciously.

After many months of instruction, I felt confident enough to attempt my first patch. Hoping to surprise and please the master, I did my work secretly. I wrote a patch that reworked several lines, reassembled the program, and released the new program to the production system.

The next morning I came in a little late. Much to my surprise, the director of the development center was in the master's office, along with the personnel director. The personnel director saw me as I walked up the hall and closed the door. I heard loud voices but could not understand what was said.

I waited until the visitors had left and then went into the master's office. "Well?" I asked.

"Your patch was brought up on the production machine at exactly 6 PM yesterday evening. It has now been removed."

"And?"

"You still have your job," the master said.

At last I understood the total futility of my efforts to understand the Code with my rational mind, and with this came a great sense of despair. Sensing this change, the master began teaching me secret

techniques of meditation and debugging, techniques that he
claimed had been handed down
from support group to support
group since the dawn of the computer age.

And as I listened, I came to realize
a great truth about my prior experiences with programming. In college, I had thought that the main
task of the programmer was to
control the workings of the hardware and software, and that the
highest art of programming was
the successful application of good
programming techniques to accomplish an assignment or goal.

But program maintenance is not like program development. To maintain a program is to treat it like a growing plant. It avails nothing to pull and tug at a shoot in an attempt to make it grow faster. In fact, such activity usually serves to kill the plant. A program must be nurtured carefully. Before one makes changes, one must be familiar with every convolution of logic and possess a deep understanding of the program's purpose. This understanding does not come overnight, but is built up over time.

After many months, I was at last able to make successful patches to

the Code, but only after long sessions of meditation, the listings propped open on my desk. I also found that it was easier to concentrate if I burnt some incense as I worked, never forgetting to repeat the mantra that the master taught me: "Null-So-Stix-Etx-Eot," which he said signified the five-fold beginning of the universe.

And soon I found that I no longer cared whether I received credit for my work, nor did I see any separation between myself and the programs that I maintained. And like a man who has lived in shadow all his life, I began to understand the Zen of programming, the ineffible and indescribable power that

lies behind all programming, like a sun that casts shadows on the earth.

Freed from the meaningless promptings of my ego, I came to realize that those mighty lines of programming had only seemed obscure to me because I had not yet become enlightened enough to understand them. I now knew why the ancient programmers had never documented their programs, for an English language description would have been more confusing than enlightening.

Then one day, I found myself working on a problem that dealt with the most complex part of the

Code — the error analysis routines. Without knowing it, I issued a patch that determined an error condition from an examination of the contents of the hardware trap area, allowing the program to continue execution correctly.

That afternoon, for the first time, the·master programmer entered my cubicle. He put his hand upon my shoulder and looked down at me. "Time for you to leave," he said.

Such was my first experience with Zen programming. Though I have been assigned to many projects since that time, I never forgot the teachings of my first master.

Imagine my surprise, then, when I
discovered so many of the master's favorite sayings in *The Zen of
Programming*! At last I began to
see the ancient traditions that lay
behind his unforgettable teachings.

The world owes a debt to Mr.
James for his rediscovery of that
classic and seminal work, which
but for his perseverence might
have been lost forever. Mr. James
has collected in this volume a
treasure trove of the peripheral
koans, tales, and poems that com-
prise the outer teachings of the
legendary "Integration Sect." It is
through the efforts of scholars

such as Mr. James that the immortal light of enlightened programming will shine upon future generations of humanware.

Charlie (Chuck) Babbage

Book One \ Wood

Master:	Ninjei
Medium:	Chronicle
Kanji:	歴史
Hardware:	Keyboard
Direction:	East
Software:	Editor
Sense:	Touch
Phase:	Interface
Beast:	Dragon
System:	VMS

Wood

The master Ninjei is best known as the reviver of the MRVMS/III-X school of Zen. According to the legends, Ninjei rose from the lowest ranks of the programmers to become the head of development for a large programming organization. He subsequently disappeared after he had completed work on an advanced operating system that (so he claimed) required neither hardware nor software to function correctly. His current whereabouts are unknown, but it is said that he appears from time to time in the guise of a management consultant.

One

When he first came to work at the development center, Ninjei was assigned to support the operating system. One day a manager came into Ninjei's cubicle.

"Why are you not working?" asked the manager.

"The system has crashed," said Ninjei.

The manager frowned. "You are paid to keep the system running!" he exclaimed.

"The system has not crashed," said Ninjei.

Two

Thus spake the Master Ninjei:

"If your application does not run correctly, do not blame the operating system."

歴史

Three

The master Ninjei went to a computer trade show.

Many companies were there with bright displays, flaxen-haired models in three-piece suits, and all the latest and greatest hardware they could muster.

Ninjei did not even glance at the other booths. Instead, he merely opened a folding chair and sat quietly in a corner. From time to time, people would wander by and ask him a question. He thought for a while, and then answered in short and simple sentences.

Three

Sitting cross-legged around him,
their gathered brochures cast aside,
the people waited in silence for
the master to speak.

歷史

Four

Thus spake the Master Ninjei:

"To the intelligent man, one
word, to the fleet horse, one flick
of the whip, to the well-written
program, a single command."

Five

The Master Ninjei went to a meeting of the board of directors.
When he began to explain about the technical characteristics of the software, the executives fidgeted in their seats, gazed out the window, and stared at their coffee cups.

So the master began talking of how much money the software would make, whereupon the executives pricked up their ears and began frisking about the room, evidently absorbed by the pleasing sounds.

Six

An executive went to see Ninjei and noticed that the master was playing a computer game. "What is the meaning of this?" demanded the executive.

"I am testing the system," said the master.

When the executive looked closely at the screen he saw that it was true.

Seven

One day the board of directors gathered together to discuss the status of the business. They called the master Ninjei in to give a report. "What is your quarterly forecast?" they asked.

"There is no quarterly forecast," Ninjei replied.

"Then what is your budget for this year?" they asked.

"There is no budget for this year," Ninjei replied.

Then they asked, "Are you certain that you are the master Ninjei?"

Seven

"There is no Ninjei," Ninjei replied.

Confused, the directors suspended their meeting and returned to their homes.

歴史

Eight

Thus spake the Master Ninjei:

"To program a million-line operating system is easy; to change a man's temperament is more difficult."

歴史

Nine

Three corporate executives from three different computer companies went to Ninjei to learn the secret of true leadership.

Ninjei asked the first executive, "Do you have the current organization chart for your company?"

The first executive pulled a piece of paper from his pocket. "I keep one with me all the time," he said, handing the paper to Ninjei.

Ninjei looked at the paper with interest. "This appears to have been created on a computer," he remarked.

Nine

"Yes indeed," said the first executive proudly, "We have computerized our organization charts so that they can be altered at a moment's notice."

Ninjei smiled and handed the paper back. "There is nothing I can do to help you," he said.

The second executive then asked Ninjei the secret of true leadership.

"Do you have the current organization chart for your company?" asked Ninjei.

The second executive shook his head. "The organization has not

Nine

changed in several years. I memorized it long ago."

Ninjei frowned. "There is nothing I can do to help you," he said.

The third executive asked Ninjei the secret of true leadership.

"Do you have the current organization chart for your company?" asked Ninjei.

The third executive shrugged. "We do not have an organization chart," he said, "Each person accomplishes the tasks that seem best at the time."

Nine

Ninjei furrowed his brows. "There is nothing I can do to help you," he said.

The three executives went aside and whispered among themselves. Returning to Ninjei, they said: "All right then, show us YOUR organization chart!"

Ninjei led them to a field where a single tree was growing out of the ground. "This is my organization chart," said Ninjei, placing his hand upon the rough surface of the bark.

歴史

Book Two \ Fire

Master:	Noa-Op
Medium:	Folktale
Kanji:	昔話
Hardware:	Monitor
Direction:	South
Software:	Formatter
Sense:	Sight
Phase:	Design
Beast:	Phoenix
System:	CP-6

Fire

The Master Noa-Op was a collector of folktales about various development projects. Recent compu-archeological research has revealed that the folktales in this volume are based upon historical fact. Although a certain amount of exaggeration may have been inadvertantly added, the core of historical truth remains.

One

When Prince Xuan staffed his software projects, he would hire three hundred programmers on a single day. A scholar who had a Ph.D. in computer science asked for a place in the company and was granted a well-paying position.

One day the Prince Xuan was deposed by the Warlord Min. "I believe in individual accountability," declared Lord Min as he reviewed his troops. Hearing this, the scholar quietly slipped away.

昔 話

Two

Two programmers were arguing about user interface.

"Significant inroads are being made in 'ease-of-use'," said the first programmer, "Soon people will no longer need to read tedious manuals before they can use a computer. Programs will be self-evident."

The second programmer thought about this for a moment and then said, "Last weekend I decided to chop some wood for a fire, but my old axe was dull and worn. So I went to the hardware store and purchased a new one."

Two

"That's all very interesting," said the first programmer, "but what does it have to do with user interface?"

"The new axe came with an eight-page instruction booklet," he replied.

昔 話

Three

A Sage once asked an Engineer, a Mathematician, a Physicist, and a Programmer: "How many sides are there to a box?"

The Engineer replied first. "There are four sides to a box," he said.

"Why do you say this?" asked the Sage.

"The four uprights are the sides, which are joined together by a top and a bottom," replied the Engineer.

"That is ridiculous," remarked the Mathematician, "A box has six sides."

Three

"Why do you say this?" asked the Sage.

"A box is a cubiform, therefore it has six sides," the Mathematician replied.

"That is untrue," said the Physicist, "A box has twelve sides."

"Why do you say this?" asked the Sage.

"Strictly speaking, there are six sides on the exterior and six sides on the interior," replied the Physicist.

The Sage looked at the Programmer, who as yet had said nothing.

Three

"What is your opinion?" inquired the Sage.

"There are only two sides to a box," said the Programmer.

At this the Engineer, Mathematician and Physicist began to laugh.

"Why do you say that there are only two sides?" asked the Sage when the laughter ceased.

"This is based upon personal experience," said the Programmer, "The 'Inside' is where the circuit boards are mounted. The 'Outside' is where you put the monitor and the keyboard."

"Exactly so," said the Sage.

昔 話

Four

A newly-appointed director was holding a get-acquainted meeting for the programmers.

In the midst of the revelry, a programmer recited the following speech: "We have looked forward to your arrival with anticipation. Your predecessor had none of your exalted ability. Now that you are here, we can become truly productive."

The new director was highly flattered. "Did you write that speech yourself?" he asked.

"It is a custom of the development center," said the programmer, "to give that speech whenever a new director arrives. It is the only speech I know."

昔話

52

Five

One day a programmer at the development center discovered an algorithm that would create mazes. Being industrious, he modified the algorithm so that it would create a single continuous maze on long strips of printer paper.

Soon he had generated a maze containing several million paths, 40 feet long and seven feet high. He hung the maze in a long hallway across from the programmers' offices. Soon the entire programming staff was crowded in front of the maze trying to solve the titanic puzzle.

Five

The director of the development center happened by and stared at the scene in sad dismay. But when he went to master programmer's office to ask advice, the master was not there.

昔話

Six

Five novices went into the master's office crying, "Woe, woe! We have heard that our project may be cancelled."

The master said, "All things continue until they stop."

Hearing this, the novices returned to work.

昔話

Seven

One day the development center received news that a new director was to be appointed over them, a warlord who knew little about computers.

Appalled by the news, the programmers stopped coding, but instead spent many hours speculating about evil days to come.

Seeing this, a master decided that something had to be done. So he rented a gorilla suit.

Presently the new director reported for duty. He gathered together all the managers into the small conference room, along with several corporate executives sent

Seven

from headquarters to "smooth the transition" as the saying was.

Suddenly the master, dressed in the gorilla suit, burst through the door. He leapt upon the conference table and kicked the papers around, and growled at the executives, who just sat there mouths agape. Then he left as suddenly as he came.

Upon hearing of this event, the programmers returned to work.

(Special Note from the Editor)
The editor has spoken with several people who witnessed the events described in this folktale.

Seven

The editor has also heard that a similar act of defiance took place at an IBM facility about a year later. This second incident was somewhat different than the first in that the programmer wore a sports jacket, stood in the doorway and coughed loudly.

昔 話

Eight

A group of programmers were presenting a report to the Emperor. "What was the greatest achievement of the year?" the Emperor asked.

The programmers spoke among themselves and then replied, "We fixed 50% more bugs this year than we fixed last year."

The Emperor looked on them in confusion. It was clear that he did not know what a "bug" was. After conferring in low undertones with his chief minister, he turned to the programmers, his face red with anger. "You are guilty of poor quality control. Next year there will be no 'bugs'!" he demanded.

Eight

And sure enough, when the programmers presented their report
to the Emperor the next year, there
was no mention of bugs.

昔話

Nine

A corporate executive came to visit the development center. Like a general reviewing his troops, he walked the long corridors, stopping here and there to talk with the people that he met. Eventually, he wandered into the office of a programmer, who as it happened was in deep concentration, debugging the operating system.

The executive glanced about the room and noticed a statue of a pig that was perched upon the programmer's terminal. "I have always been fascinated by the curios and mementos that programmers collect," said the executive, "they always seem to have some interesting tale behind them. For exam-

Nine

ple, what is the meaning of that
sculpture there?" He pointed at
the statue.

The programmer looked up from
his terminal, blinked, and then
stared at the statue as if he were
seeing it for the first time. "It's a
pig," he said.

昔 話

The Zen of Programming

○

Book Three \ Earth

Master:	Rinzai
Medium:	Analect
Kanji:	俳句
Hardware:	CPU
Direction:	Center
Software:	Debugger
Sense:	Smell
Phase:	Coding
Beast:	Ox
System:	OS/VS

Earth

The Master Rinzai, author of the following analects, remains a shadowy figure. Little is known about him other than that he was assassinated by agents of the COBOL standards committee.

One

Thus I have heard:

Things that seem easy in the beginning often prove the most difficult at the end. That is why programmers say, "It will take half the time to develop the first 90 percent, and the other half to develop the last 10 percent."

俳句

Two

Thus I have heard:

The greatest mistake made in Computer/Human interfaces is the denial of the computer. Systems that are backfitted to previous conceptions of the universe are always limited by what has gone before. Computers should not simulate reality — they should transcend it.

俳句

Three

Thus I have heard:

A computer company designed a powerful system that was ahead of its time. Because they were afraid that the new design might be copied they kept the architecture of the hardware secret and made certain that the operating system was proprietary.

Ten years later, a novice asked the master programmer about the dusty old crate that was sitting in the back of the data center.

俳句

Four

Thus I have heard:

Never make a technical decision based upon the politics of the situation. Never make a political decision based upon technical issues. The only place where these realms meet is in the mind of the unenlightened.

俳句

Five

Thus I have heard:

Project plans and published schedules have no meaning within themselves. The dates and milestones upon them are essentially meaningless. But there is a secret schedule that is understood by all who work upon a project. This secret schedule is never fooled by outside concerns, it is never manipulated to satisfy a marketing group. The secret schedule is always followed because it reflects the understanding between all members of the development team. When project plans reflect this reality, then programs are delivered on time. When project plans contradict this reality, then programs are delivered late.

俳句

Six

Thus I have heard:

There are three conditions that guarantee the failure of a programming project. The first condition is that the managers in control of the project know nothing about software. The second condition is that the project leaders responsible for the code have no interest in writing the code. The third condition is that programmers who are to write the code are contracted and thus have no loyalty to the project. Any one of these conditions can doom a project to failure; all three together are certain death.

俳句

Seven

Thus I have heard:

Many executives delight in organization charts that show them at the top of the heap, with their "subordinates" beneath them. Is it then surprising that so many executives resemble nothing more than children playing at "king on the mountain"? Organization charts are sometimes called "tree-structures;" but the executives who use them always seem to forget that the only tree that has its leaves on the bottom is one that has been uprooted and hence can no longer live. The superior executive considers himself at the bottom of the organization, accepting the burden of leadership because it is the best way for him to serve.

Seven

This is the meaning of the famous parable about Master Ninjei — he could not teach the secret of leadership because his would-be students believed too strongly in the myth of their own power. When an organization is led well, the employees do not even know that they are being led. When the project is finished, they say to themselves: "Look at what we have accomplished by our own efforts!"

俳句

Eight

Thus I have heard:

The worth of a program cannot be judged by the size of its brochures or by the number of full-page ads that appear in popular computer magazines. The louder the noise, the less likely it is that the program will be useful. Truly excellent programs need no advertising; word of mouth is sufficient.

俳句

Nine

Thus I have heard:

There is a cycle, a rhythm to the universe. Today one program will be popular, tomorrow another. Today 500 bugs will be fixed, tomorrow another 500 will appear. To understand Life is to know that the rhythm exists. To understand Zen is to live outside this rhythm, detached from the everyday concerns of life. Only then can the mind be free.

俳句

Book Four \ Metal

Master:	Lan-Hsi
Medium:	Koan
Kanji:	講話
Hardware:	Printer
Direction:	West
Software:	Interpreter
Sense:	Hearing
Phase:	Debugging
Beast:	Rabbit
System:	MS-DOS

Metal

The Master Lan-Hsi tended to teach using the koan — a teaching device unique to Zen. Often the meaning of an individual koan is difficult to resolve and frequently there are several inner and outer meanings.

The Zen of Programming

One

A novice who had studied long at the university went to see the master programmer.

The novice said: "I have memorized the collected algorithms of the ACM, all twelve volumes of 'The Art of Computer Programming', and I can program in LISP, PROLOG, SNOBOL, ALGOL, MODULA2, and ADA."

The master nodded politely. "It is seldom that I meet a man as erudite as yourself," he said, "I would like your opinion of a program that I have written."

One

"I would be happy to assist you," said the novice, throwing his chest out with pride.

The master went to his personal computer and inserted a diskette. "First I must make a copy," he explained.

They sat there for a few minutes, listening to the rustle of the spinning drive. Suddenly the computer displayed a message reading "No more space on disk...Abort, Retry, or Ignore?"

The master programmer typed "R" to retry the operation. Once more they listened to the drive

One

and once more the error message appeared upon the screen. But the master merely pressed "R" once more, repeating the same sequence of events.

Finally the novice could restrain himself no longer. "There is no more room on the diskette!" he said angrily, "It is too full!"

The master said: "It is your mind that is too full."

And then the novice was enlightened.

講話

Two

Thus spake the master: "Any program, no matter how small, contains bugs."

The novice did not believe the master's words. "What if the program were so small that it performed but a single function?" he asked.

"Such a program would have no meaning," said the master, "but if such a one existed, the operating system would fail eventually, producing a bug."

But the novice was not satisfied. "What if the operating system did not fail?" he asked.

Two

"There is no operating system that does not fail," said the master, "but if such a one existed, the hardware would fail eventually, producing a bug."

The novice still was not satisfied. "What if the hardware did not fail?" he asked.

The master gave a great sigh. "There is no hardware that does not fail," he said, "but if such a one existed, the user would want the program to do something different, and this too is a bug.

A program without bugs would be an absurdity, a nonesuch. If there were a program without any bugs then the world would cease to exist."

講話

Three

The Magician of the Ivory Tower-
visited the master programmer,
bringing his latest
invention as usual.

The master programmer looked
up from his terminal and saw the
magician standing in the doorway.
"What have you brought this
time?" asked the master.

"This is my greatest invention,"
said the magician, wheeling a box
into the room, "It is the ultimate
desktop publishing system. With
it I do everything that can be accomplished with a typesetter, a
light table, and a camera. I have
designed it so that anyone familiar
with traditional printing can learn
to use the software in a few
months. A programmer can learn

Three

it in twice that time. Here is a sample page I have generated. Behold: it resembles the first page of the Guttenberg Bible!"

The master programmer examined the sample output, a slight smile on his face. "What is the anticipated usage for the device?" he asked.

"We will use it for technical publishing," said the magician.

(Special Note from the Editor)

The magician is often used in Zen folktales to introduce antithetical

Three

circumstances. It is not known if this personage actually existed. However there are legends to the effect that the tower was manned by a legion of fanatical devotees who were persuaded to commit software piracy, murder, and various other unethical acts in return for machine time on a Cray-2.

The tower was besieged and nearly destroyed at the end of the third dynasty but was salvaged and restored by a government grant.

講話

Four

A novice went into the master's cubicle and saw a new computer sitting upon the master's desk.

"What is that computer?" asked the novice.

The master placed his hand upon a small box that was connected to the computer by a wire. "Behold," said the master, "This device controls what we see on the screen."

The novice looked closely at the screen, but all he saw were meaningless symbols.

"The screen simulates a desk," explained the master, "For example,

Four

here on the screen is a filing cabi-
net and a trash repository. Here
also is a typewriter and a calcula-
tor."

"This is a wonderful invention,"
whispered the novice in awe.

"It is not as wonderful as it
seems," said the master. He took
the novice by the shoulders and
made him stand several feet back.
"Can you see the two desks?"
asked the master.

The novice nodded. "One is on
the floor, the other is on the
screen," he remarked.

Four

"Just so. Now, is there something missing on one of the two desks?"

The novice pondered for a moment. "One of the desks does not have a computer on it," he said.

The master shook his head. "Neither of the desks has a computer on it."

講話

Five

A novice asked the master: "What is the true meaning of programming?"

The master replied: "Eat when you are hungry, sleep when you are fatigued, program when the moment is right."

講話

Six

Hearing a disturbance, The master programmer went into the novice's cubicle.

"Curse these personal computers!" cried the novice in anger, "To make them do anything I must use three or even four editing programs. Sometimes I get so confused that I erase entire files. This is truly intolerable!"

The master programmer stared at the novice. "And what would you do to remedy this state of affairs?" he asked.

The novice thought for a moment. "I will design a new editing

Six

program," he said, "a program that will replace all these others."

Suddenly the master struck the novice on the side of his head. It was not a heavy blow, but the novice was nonetheless surprised. "What did you do that for?" exclaimed the novice.

"I have no wish to learn another editing program," said the master.

And suddenly the novice was enlightened.

講話

Seven

A novice asked the master, "Whenever I program on a new system I must learn a new language. Why are there no standards?"

The master turned away. "The only true standard is Death," he said.

講話

Eight

A novice asked the master: "Is there Buddha-nature in an ADA compiler?"

The master replied: "Have you ever noticed that the NUL character is 000 in both octal, hex, and decimal?"

Suddenly the novice was enlightened.

講話

Nine

Two programmers named Diagu
and Gudo were making presenta-
tins to the president of a large cor-
poration.

When he stood up to speak, Gudo
said to the executive, "You are
wise by nature and understand the
true meaning of computers."

"Nonsense," said Diagu, "Why do
you praise this fool? He may be an
executive, but he knows nothing
about computers."

The executive rewarded them
both and then hired a consultant
to determine which of them was
correct.

講話

The Zen of Programming

Book Five \ Water

Master:	Yoshiko
Medium:	Haiku
Kanji:	説教
Hardware:	Disk
Direction:	North
Software:	Compiler
Sense:	Taste
Phase:	Testing
Beast:	Snake
System:	Unix

Water

The Zen Nun Yoshiko primarily wrote haiku — short poems that attempt to express a feeling or idea in a predefined set of syllables. Haiku expresses much about the lonely life a programmer leads: the late nights spent debugging, the thankless toil of testing, the simple joy of watching a program compile. All programmers share such experiences, though they seldom speak of them, even among themselves.

The final selection of this book is evidently a fragment of a larger work. The editor begs the indulgence of the reader for his inability to translate the profound concepts of these poems in their full and original resonance.

One

Programs are but dreams
Born in formless, shapeless Zen.
We are but dreamers.

説教

Two

I programmed three days
And heard no human voices.
But the hard disk sang.

説教

Three

The compiler runs
Like a swift-flowing river.
I wait in silence.

説教

Four

Why do you use LISP?
I understand COBOL not.
Therefore I use LISP.

説教

Five

I programmed all night.
Through the window, on my screen,
The rising sun shined.

説教

Six

Hardware and software,
We are your slaves and masters,
Our lives are programs.

説教

Seven

Can you hear the sound
Of a program on the disk?
The answer is NUL.

説教

Eight

I read my E-Mail.
The project has been cancelled.
Purging files, I weep.

説教

Nine

The computer center is empty,
Silent except for the whine of the
cooling fans.
I walk the rows of CPUs,
My skin prickling with magnetic
flux.
I open a door, cold and hard,
And watch the lights dancing on
the panels.
A machine without soul, men call
it,
But its soul is the sweat of my
comrades,
Within it lie the years of our lives,
Disappointment, friendship, sad
ness, joy,
The algorithmic exultations,
The long nights filled with thank
less toil,

Nine

I hear the echoes of sighs and
   laughter,
And in the darkened offices
The terminals shine like stars.

説教

About The Author

Geoffrey James is a *magna cum laude* graduate of the University of California and has been a software engineer for a major computer manufacturer since 1977.

In 1984 he received a technical excellence award for the design and implementation of an advanced computer-aided publishing system. He also lectures and teaches University level courses on computer-aided publishing systems.

He is author of *Enochian Evocation* (a translation / transcription of a 16th-century proto-scientific manuscript) and *Document Databases* (a comprehensive study of

automated publications methodology). *Document Databases* is recognized as the outstanding text in the field of online documentation and electronic publishing.

And, of course, Mr. James is the author of the now famous classic *The Tao of Programming* — also published by InfoBooks.

A student for many years of Tai Chi, Mr. James appreciates the oriental philosophies and applies their principles in his daily life.

About This Book

We enjoyed making this book for you.

Our intention is to share with you the joy of those singular moments of discovery and awareness when we truly know and feel ourselves.

Because true awareness rides on the softly curved canoe of a smile, we offer our little book to you supported by the loving, easy, flowing waters of humor.

The Zen of Programming is a companion text to *The Tao of Programming* — also written by Geoffrey James and published by InfoBooks.

This book was electronically formatted and adjusted on the Macintosh computer

and typeset on a LaserWriter, using Palatino for the body text and Avant Garde for the running heads and display type.

The Japanese calligraphy, drawn by Teri Fujikawa, accurately translates the five parts of this book — Wood, Fire, Earth, Metal, and Water. Also, the calligraphy used to indicate the end of each selection accurately translates what kind of a selection it is — see the Table "How This Book Is Organized" on page x.

As with *The Tao of Programming*, we have combined selected Analects and Haiku poems along with illustrations from the text and reproduced them as attractive posters; so you and your friends can have your favorite selections decorating your home or office. Write to us for our catalog.

Other Titles Available From:
InfoBooks
P.O. Box 1018
Santa Monica, California 90406
213-470-6786

	Please send me the following books		
No.	Title	Unit Price	Extended Price
	The Writer's Pocket Almanack	$ 7.95	
	Your Best Interest	$ 9.95	
	The Tao of Programming	$ 7.95	
	The Zen of Programming	$ 7.95	
	Book Catalog	FREE	
	Tao and Zen Poster Catalog	FREE	

Taxes: In California please add 6.5% sales tax.
Shipping: $1.50 first book; $1.00 each additional book for surface mail.
$.2.50 first book; $2.00 each additional book for first class.

Ship To:

Name_____

Company_____

Address_____

City_____State_____Zip_____

Telephone _____

Thank You For Your Order